Me
Town

This bound edition published in the UK by Scholastic, 2025
Scholastic, Bosworth Avenue, Warwick, CV34 6UQ
Scholastic Ireland, 89E Lagan Road, Dublin Industrial Estate, Glasnevin, Dublin, D11 HP5F

First published in the ANZ by Scholastic Australia, 2024

Book design by Laura Ye.

ISBN 978 0702 34446 6

A CIP catalogue record for this book is available from the British Library.

Printed in China
Paper made from wood grown in sustainable forests and other controlled sources.

FSC www.fsc.org MIX Paper | Supporting responsible forestry FSC® C008047

10 9 8 7 6 5 4 3 2 1

www.scholastic.co.uk

For safety or quality concerns:
UK: www.scholastic.co.uk/productinformation
EU: www.scholastic.ie/productinformation

Meow Town

Rebecca McRitchie

Erin Hunting

For Evie, Max, Teddy and Sophia-RM

To Cassie Anne, my dreamer.
Thank you for your never-ending support-EH

Chapter 1

Bella the kitty cat **raced** through Meow Town. Today was a good day. It was a good day because Bella had the most purrfect idea ever! Her tail wiggled with excitement. She couldn't wait to tell her **friends** her idea.

But where were her friends?

Bella ran over and looked by the water bowl fountain. But her friends weren't there.

Bella darted between the houses of **Meow Town**.

She looked in the cake shop. But they weren't there, either.

She bounded over Windmill Bridge and leaped over the stepping-stone path of Squeaky Creek.

Then Bella turned a corner, and at last she **spotted** her friends. They were lying outside on the grass by the pond. It was one of the **nicest** places in all of Meow Town.

Margo, Pickles and Abby Tabby were Bella's best friends.

Margo loved pretty and sparkly things. And today, she wore a pair of pointy sunglasses and was brushing her long, soft fur by the pond.

Pickles loved collecting things. Socks, feathers, lint, rocks and bugs.

Today, she was trying to catch a **cricket** in the grass for her bug collection.

Abby Tabby loved… doing **nothing**. Today, the big, stripy cat was napping in the sunshine.

And Bella loved to go on **adventures**!

"I just had the **best** idea for what we can do today!" Bella said when she reached her friends by the pond.

"Is it to go shopping?" Margo asked excitedly. "I need a new brush."

"You already have lots of fur brushes," said Pickles. "Five of them."

"No," said Bella. "That's not my idea."

"Is it to lie here in the sun?" murmured Abby Tabby. Then she stretched out and started to fall back to sleep.

"Nope," said Bella. She paused for suspense. Then she said loudly, "My idea is to go—"

"Please tell me you're not going on an adventure," came a **sly** voice from the shadows of a tree.

Bella stopped. Her tail twitched. She knew who the voice belonged to. Bella turned, crossing her paws over her chest.

"What do you want, Seth?"

Slinking over to them were not one but two *hairless kitty cats* – Seth and Fluffy. They were always together, and they always enjoyed causing **trouble**.

"Don't you know that adventures are for dogs, not cats?" said Seth.

"Yeah," said Fluffy. "And you are cats."

"Adventures can be for *anyone,*" said Margo, glaring at the pair from behind her sunglasses.

"You're not brave enough for adventures," said Seth.

"You'll probably get – HICCUP! – lost," said Fluffy, letting out a surprise hiccup.

"Or nibbled by the **foxes**," added Seth.

"Nibbled?" squeaked Pickles. "Foxes?"

Seth laughed. Fluffy **hiccupped**.

"The foxes have been gone for months," said Abby Tabby, sitting up.

"I heard they've been seen in the Mud Woods," said Seth.

"Yeah," said Fluffy. "They looked really scary."

Bella paused. "Wait, you've seen them?" she said. "You're supposed to report any fox sightings to the mayor."

Seth nudged Fluffy in the ribs.

"Uh, I mean... no," Fluffy said. She hiccupped again. "It must have been a pair of orange… rocks."

Then the hairless cats raced off, heading in the direction of Furry Purry Hill.

Bella and her friends watched as the cats disappeared.

"That was weird," said Abby Tabby.

"Never mind them," Bella said. "Let's go pack for our adventure!"

Chapter 2

At home, the kitty cats planned their **adventure**. With her special adventure hat on, Bella pointed to her map of Meow Town.

"We can start here at Squeaky Creek and go this way towards the **Mud Woods**," suggested Bella.

"But the Mud Woods are at the edge of Meow Town," said Pickles. "We've *never* been that far."

"That's what makes it an adventure, Pickles," Bella said happily.

"Is there mud in the Mud Woods?" Margo asked. "Should I bring paw mittens?"

"Only one way to find out," said Bella. "And, if we go this way to Furry Purry Hill, we should be back home in time for dinner," said Bella.

"That sounds **delicious**," said Abby Tabby.

Excited, Bella raced around the house and put all the things she would need for the adventure in her backpack. But when she had finished...

Margo, Pickles and Abby Tabby were not ready at all!

"I don't know about going on an adventure today," said Pickles, **worried**.

Bella saw that Pickles had only packed one thing in her purple backpack. A sock. Not a *pair* of socks. Just one *single* sock. And it had a hole in it.

"We should really leave now while there is plenty of sunlight," Bella said. She made her way to the door.

"Where are my pink, sparkly paw mittens?!" said Margo. She had pulled out *all* of her drawers and was rummaging through them.

"There they are," said Abby Tabby, pointing to a pair of paw mittens underneath a yellow scarf.

Margo picked them up. "These are not pink and sparkly, Abby Tabby. These are quite clearly green and woolly!"

Abby Tabby shrugged.

"I simply *can't* go on an adventure without my pink sparkly mittens," said Margo.

"Maybe we *shouldn't* go," said Pickles. "You heard what Seth and Fluffy said," she added, "about the **foxes**."

"They just wanted to be **meanies**," Bella

said. She glanced at the clock. "It's getting late. We really need to go now," Bella said impatiently, marching towards the door.

"Hold on, Bella," Margo said. "We're not ready yet."

Bella noticed that Abby Tabby's backpack was still hung up on a hook behind the door, empty. Pickles was trying to fit her rock collection into her backpack. And Margo had a big pile of clothes on the floor next to her.

Bella's fur stuck up. Her friends were taking **way too long**. She didn't want to miss out on having an adventure.

She let out a small **huff**, then she put on her backpack and set off on the adventure by herself.

Chapter 3

Bella **pounced** happily through Meow Town. This was it. She was on an adventure.

She stopped and smelled some yellow flowers. They tickled her nose.

'ACHOO!' Bella sneezed.

She ran up a hill and then she rolled down a hill. She chased a butterfly.

Bella made her way over Squeaky Creek. As she walked, the sunshine felt nice on her fur. And she could hear birds singing in the trees.

Then Bella turned in the direction of the Mud Woods. She could see the big trees up ahead.

When she got there, Bella paused. The woods looked darker and a little scarier than she'd imagined. But then she remembered what Seth said about cats not being brave enough for adventures.

Bravely, Bella made her way inside the Mud Woods.

SPLOSH!

Bella's paws landed in mud.

As she walked, the Mud Woods got darker and colder and muddier.

"Yuck!" said Bella. Her fur was now covered in mud.

Bella trudged and trudged through the Mud Woods. Then she paused. Was she going the right way? Should she go left? Or right? Each way she turned looked exactly the same.

"Oh no," said Bella. "I think I'm lost."

That's when Bella saw a pretty pink flower poking out of the trees. It reminded her of Margo.

Then a cricket hopped past her, bouncing through the mud, and it reminded her of Pickles.

Nearby, Bella saw a small patch of grass with a little bit of sunlight. It would be the perfect spot for Abby Tabby to take a nap.

Bella sighed.

She wished she had waited for her friends. If only she had been more patient.

Then Bella heard a **rustling** in the prickly bushes ahead of her. She stopped. What was that? What if it's... what if it's...

Out of the top of the bushes, she saw a pair of orange-and-black tails. Orange-and-black tails that could only belong to...

Bella gasped.

The foxes!

Chapter 4

Bella turned and ran through the Mud Woods as quickly as she could. She raced and raced, jumping over puddles and sliding under tree branches… until she bumped into something soft and fluffy.

'OOF!'

Bella looked up and saw that it was…
"Margo! Abby Tabby! Pickles!" she exclaimed.

"We found you!" said Pickles.

Bella was so happy to see her friends. She gave them a big hug.

Bella realized she owed her friends an apology. "I'm sorry I wasn't patient," she said. Then she remembered the foxes. "But we need to leave now!"

"But we just got here," said Pickles.

"It's the foxes," whispered Bella, looking at the way she had come.

Nearby, two orange-and-black tails stuck up out of the bushes. They were coming **closer** and **closer** to the kitty cats.

Pickles gasped. "What do we do?"

But then they heard something else.

There was a growl. And then...

HICCUP!

Bella looked at her friends.

"Wait a minute," whispered Abby Tabby.

"Wasn't Fluffy **hiccupping** earlier?" Pickles said softly.

Margo squinted at the fox tails. "I think some mean kitty cats are playing a trick." She pointed to a hairless paw they could see under the bushes.

It was Seth and Fluffy! They were pretending to be foxes!

Bella had an idea. "Follow my lead," she said. She puffed out her chest and said loudly, "Oh no, not foxes!"

They heard a snigger and a soft hiccup from the bushes.

"Whatever will we do?" Margo said in her best **acting voice**.

Pickles pointed next to her. There was a muddy hill that went all the way down into a mud pool at the bottom. "I really hope they don't come any closer," said Pickles even louder.

Carefully, the kitty cats moved away from the mud slide and stood by a tree.

"I hope they don't jump out of those prickly bushes," said Abby Tabby in a big voice.

Suddenly, Seth and Fluffy did just that!

They **pounced** out of the prickly bushes, dressed from head to paw as foxes.

'BOO!' they both yelled.

But Fluffy and Seth had jumped into some very, very **slippery** mud. Their legs couldn't stand still.

"It's too – **HICCUP** – slippery!" Fluffy yelled.

"Argh!" Seth cried out.

Then the pair fell over and slid all the way down the muddy hill.

They landed with a SPLAT! SPLAT! into the mud pool below.

"Scaring kitty cats isn't very nice, Seth and Fluffy," Margo said.

Seth and Fluffy looked up at them, mud dripping from their faces.

"How did you know it was us?" Fluffy said, surprised. Then she hiccupped.

Angrily, Seth splashed Fluffy with mud. "Because of you!"

"Me? It was your bad acting!" Fluffy said and splashed Seth with mud.

"It was your hiccups!" said Seth, splashing her even more.

Bella and her friends watched as Seth and Fluffy **fought** in the mud.

"Come on, kitties! We have an adventure to finish!" said Bella.

Chapter 5

Bella led the way as the kitties journeyed back through the Mud Woods.

They **trudged** further and further,

until finally, they pushed through and out on to a soft, grassy hill.

"We did it!" said Pickles. She danced on the spot.

"Piece of cake," said Margo. She lay down on the hill and soaked up the sunlight.

The kitty cats sat next to her on Furry Purry Hill and looked down at Meow Town below.

Bella smiled. What a great **adventure** they'd had! She was so glad that her friends had come to find her.

"Do you think Seth and Fluffy will find their way out?" asked Pickles.

"I think they'll be fine," said Margo, pointing down the hill.

Seth and Fluffy **tumbled** out of the Mud Woods, dripping with mud. They slipped and fell as they made their way back to Meow Town.

The kitty cats **giggled**.

"Now to plan our next adventure!" Bella said. "What will it be?"

"**Bug catching!**" said Pickles.

"**Shopping!**" said Margo

"**Sleep!**" said Abby Tabby.

Meow Town

Rebecca McRitchie

Erin Hunting

For Steven and Quinn-RM

To Louie and Astrid, my two kitty cats, who teach me how to have patience, have fun and to love unconditionally-EH

Chapter 1

Bella, Margo, Pickles and Abby Tabby are best-friend kitties who live in Meow Town. They do everything together.

They lie by the pond **together**.

They brush their fur **together**.

They bake kitty-cookies **together**.

They eat yummy fish buns **together**.

But some days are **special days**. On one special day, the best-friend kitties had decided to celebrate because… it was **Abby Tabby's birthday!**

Bella, Pickles and Margo had organised a **surprise party!** Every kitty cat in Meow Town was going to be there. The plan was to keep Abby Tabby busy while they set up the party in the town square.

The friends couldn't wait for Abby Tabby to wake up. Pickles was drawing a face on one of her rocks. Margo was organizing her drawer full of sparkly scarves. Bella was pacing around the house, watching the clock.

"It's time for Abby Tabby to wake up!" Bella said, pouncing on the spot with excitement. "It's nearly time for her surprise party!"

The kitties went and stood next to Abby Tabby's bed.

"Happy birthday!" Bella squealed.

"Happy birthday!" said Margo and Pickles.

Abby Tabby sat up with a yawn.

"Thank you!" she said. Then she gave a big long stretch.

"What do you want to do today?" Bella asked. "We can do whatever you like!"

"Let's lie by the pond," said Abby Tabby.

"Are you sure?" said Margo. "We lie by the pond all the time. Don't you want to do something special today? I could give you a fur-cut?"

"We could climb that big tree near Tumble Umble Bridge? Or we could do a puzzle before we go to your—" Pickles stopped.

"Before we go to what?" said Abby Tabby. She squinted at Pickles.

Bella and Margo looked over at Pickles, eyes wide. Pickles wasn't very good at keeping secrets.

"Um… the pond is a great idea! Let's go there now," Pickles said quickly. She put away her rocks.

"Yay!" said Abby Tabby.

Outside, the sun was shining in Meow Town. It was a very nice day for a **surprise party**.

"I'll meet you at the pond," said Bella.

"Where are you going?" Abby Tabby asked, puzzled.

Bella paused. "Um... I just want to see something."

Abby Tabby **shrugged** before walking off in the direction of the pond.

Margo and Pickles said goodbye to Bella.

Phew, thought Bella. *That was close.*

She **raced** off to set up Abby Tabby's surprise party.

Chapter 2

While Margo and Pickles were by the pond with Abby Tabby, Bella tried her best to set up the party. But it wasn't going so well.

Just when Bella finished hanging the streamers, the wind whipped up and they floated away.

Bella quickly chased after them.

She blew up the balloons, but they got **tangled** together in the gusts of wind.

"Bother! This windy day is not helping!" she said.

Bella quickly unpicked the tangles with her claws.

Then she put out the food that Margo and Pickles had been busy baking all week long. There was so much **food!**

Bella carefully laid out the buttermilk biscuits, vanilla freckle custards, rainbow ice-cream muffins, purple sprinkle doughnuts and chocolate brownie crumbles!

Then Bella got to work pumping up the jumping castle. It had a big slide on its front.

"Are we too early?" said a voice nearby.

Bella turned to see Seth and Fluffy walking over. She groaned. Seth and Fluffy were two hairless cats who also lived in Meow Town. Sometimes they were sneaky, other times they were tricky, and all the time they were up to no good.

Fluffy stuck out a claw to taste one of the rainbow ice-cream muffins.

"Not yet," said Bella, moving the yummy muffins away. "We need to wait for Abby Tabby."

"But they look so delicious," said Fluffy.

That's when Seth noticed something on the ground.

"Are you using that?" Seth asked Bella, pointing to the small ball of fur. It must have fallen from her while she was busy setting up the party.

"No," said Bella, confused. "Why?"

"No reason," said Fluffy. Then the two hairless cats quickly scooped up the fur and raced off.

"That was weird," said Bella.

She put up a big Happy Birthday sign and then she stood back, looking at her **hard work**. Some streamers had fallen down and a balloon or two had floated away, but it still looked good!

Bella couldn't wait to surprise Abby Tabby with this!

When it was time for the party, everyone in Meow Town had arrived in the town square. Mayor Whiskers was first and was followed by Lolly, who owned the bakery, carrying a tray of fish buns. Quinn, Bruno and Fern all came together. And even Jinx, who usually preferred to sit by himself and read a book, came along.

Everyone brought lovely presents for Abby Tabby.

Bella welcomed all the guests and put the gifts neatly on a table.

That's when Pickles raced over. "Bella! It's time! Abby Tabby's on her way!" she said excitedly.

"Quickly, everybody hide," said Bella to all the guests.

The kitty cats of Meow Town hid behind everything and anything they could find. Some hid behind bushes, others hid behind tables. Some hid behind the water fountain.

They all watched and waited for the **birthday kitty cat** to arrive. That's when Margo and Abby Tabby walked into the town square. And one, two, three…

'SURPRISE!'

"Happy birthday, Abby Tabby!" everyone **cheered**, jumping up out of their hiding places.

"Oh my fur," said Abby Tabby. "A surprise party!" She **waved** to all the guests.

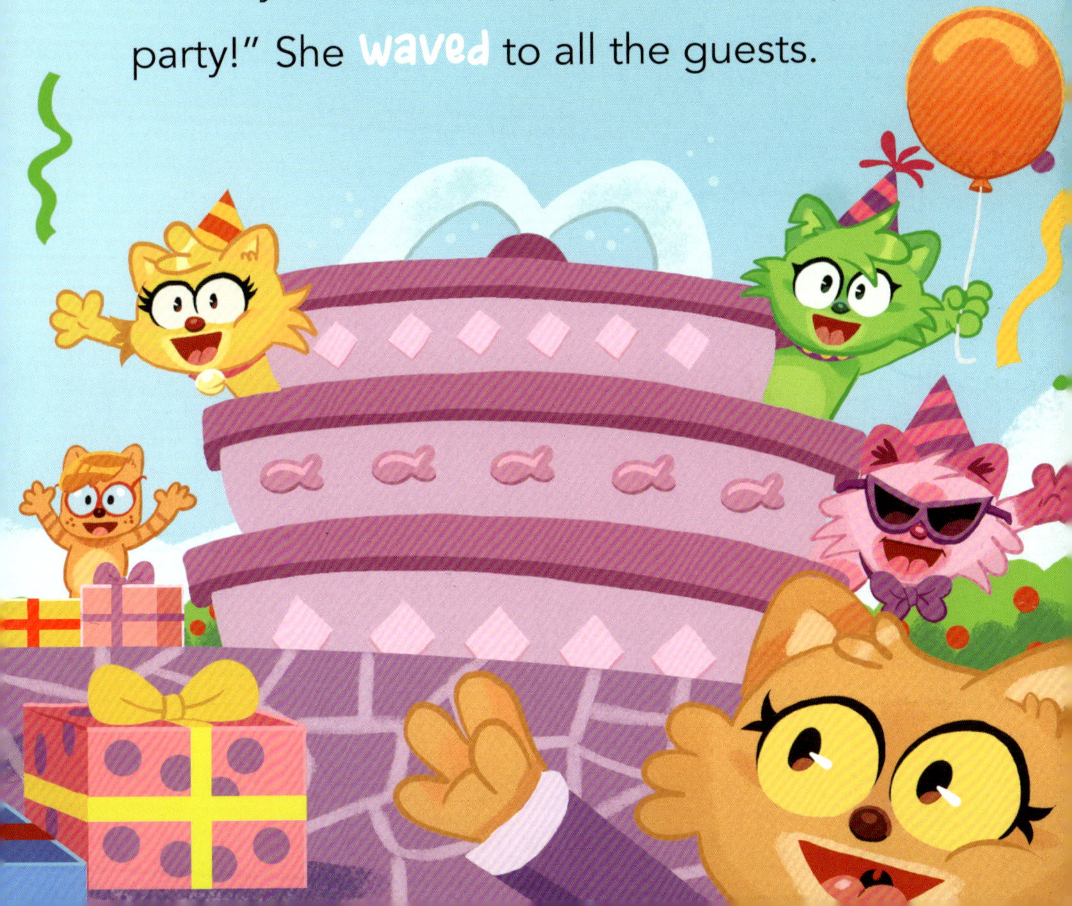

Pickles pulled out her notebook. She was in charge of the games. "The first game to play is pin the tail on the mouse," Pickles said. "Followed by musical chairs."

Abby Tabby looked so happy.

Everyone lined up for pin the tail on the mouse.

Bella was about to eat one of the rainbow ice-cream muffins when she noticed that there were two kitty cats who were missing from the party.

Seth and Fluffy.

Maybe they were still hiding? Bella looked everywhere for them. She looked near the kittycakes. She looked behind the balloons and streamers. But she couldn't see them at all.

Then Bella finally spotted them! The two hairless cats were pouncing up Furry Purry Hill.

What are they up to? Bella wondered. She looked over at Abby Tabby, Margo and Pickles. They were having lots of fun playing pin the tail on the mouse and eating kittycakes.

Bella decided to follow Seth and Fluffy by herself. If she was quick, nobody would notice she was missing from the party.

So, Bella raced up Furry Purry Hill.

Chapter 1

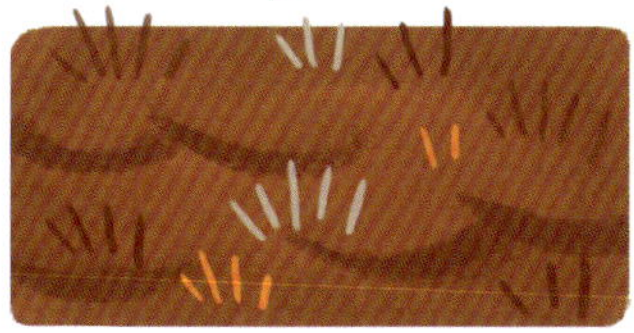

When Bella got to the top of Furry Purry Hill, she found the hairless kitty cats **whispering** to each other.

"Hello, Seth and Fluffy," Bella said. "Why are you all the way up here?"

Seth and Fluffy **jumped** in surprise.

"Nothing," said Fluffy.

"Huh?" said Bella.

"Nothing," said Seth.

Bella thought that Seth and Fluffy were acting sneakier than usual. She squinted at them suspiciously.

"Why aren't you at Abby Tabby's party? There's food and games," Bella said.

"Um," said Fluffy.

"None of your business," said Seth, crossing his arms.

"Bella, what are you doing all the way up here?" a voice called from behind them.

Bella turned to see Pickles and Margo running up Furry Purry Hill.

"We're about to cut the cake," said Margo, concerned.

"And open presents," added Pickles.

"Oh, I love cake," said Fluffy. "And presents."

Seth elbowed Fluffy.

That's when Pickles noticed something. "What is that?" she asked, pointing to something big in the tree behind Seth.

"Uh… I don't see anything," said Fluffy.

Seth stepped in front of the tree. But he was only a small cat, so he did not hide the big thing very well at all.

Bella looked up at it. Whatever it was, it was large, round and... hairy. Was this why Seth and Fluffy weren't at Abby Tabby's party?

Suddenly, a big gust of wind whipped across Furry Purry Hill. It blew and blew strongly. Seth and Fluffy looked worriedly behind them.

"Uh-oh," said Seth.

"What do you mean Uh-Oh?" Margo said.

"*Uh-oh* never means anything good," said Pickles with concern.

And that's when Bella and the kitty cats saw what Seth and Fluffy were hiding. It was…

... a giant furball! And it was the size of a house!

"Cuddly kittens!" shrieked Pickles. "Is that kitty-cat fur?"

The monster furball wobbled and rocked in the wind. And when the wind whipped up strongly again, the giant furball slowly started to roll towards them.

"Run!" said Fluffy.

Seth and Fluffy dived out of the way.

The kitty cats **Shrieked**. Then Bella, Margo and Pickles turned and ran. Together they raced down Furry Purry Hill as the furball rolled behind them.

Oh no! It was heading straight for Meow Town! And **Abby Tabby's party!**

Chapter 1

"Quick," said Bella. "We have to do something." They couldn't let the giant furball destroy Abby Tabby's party.

Bella and her friends looked behind them. The furball bounced and bumped its way down the hill, picking up speed.

"How will we stop it?" Pickles yelled.

"It's too big!" said Margo.

"And too fast!" added Bella.

The furball caught up to them as it zoomed down the hill.

Then Bella had an amazing idea!

"The jumping castle!" Bella said. "Let's push it into the furball's path."

"Good idea!" said Pickles.

The furball bounced into Meow Town and Abby Tabby's party. The kitty cats ran. The kitty cats shrieked. And when she saw it, Abby Tabby ducked for cover behind the kittycakes table.

The furball barrelled through the party,

knocking over chairs, streamers and Abby Tabby's birthday present-table.

That's when Bella and the kitty cats put their plan into action.

"Margo," said Bella. "You take that side. Pickles, you take the other side."

Together the three friends pushed the jumping castle into the path of the furball.

The furball zoomed straight towards them. Margo, Bella and Pickles dived out of the way just as the furball hit the jumping castle!

The furball **rolled** all the way up the jumping castle's bouncy slide and then—

BOING!

It bounced up into the air!

Everyone in Meow Town stopped to watch as the big furball soared across the sky above them.

Then the furball fell.

SPLOSH!

It landed right in the middle of the pond.

All the kitty cats **Cheered!** Bella and her friends looked around. There were presents and streamers on the ground, but they had mostly **saved** Abby Tabby's birthday party!

Bella, Margo and Pickles **high-fived**.

That's when Seth and Fluffy **slinked** over.

"We're sorry," said Fluffy.

"We've been **collecting** fur around Meow Town for weeks," said Seth.

"It isn't easy being the only hairless cats in Meow Town," said Seth. "It's embarrassing."

"We just wanted a nice fur scarf," added Fluffy. "It can get pretty cold on a windy day."

"I can help with that," said Margo. She raced home and came back with two sparkly scarves for Seth and Fluffy.

"Thank you," said Fluffy, trying hers on.

The kitty cats of Meow Town helped Seth and Fluffy clean up all the mess that their runaway furball had made. And soon, Meow Town was purrfect once more.

"You're just in time for cake," said Abby Tabby when they rejoined the party. She handed her friends, Fluffy and Seth a slice of blueberry cake.

Fluffy's eyes lit up.

Abby Tabby hugged her friends. "Thank you for my birthday party. And thank you for saving the day! I've had the best day ever."

Bella, Margo and Pickles were so happy. Even with a giant runaway furball, Abby Tabby's surprise birthday party was a success!

Meow Town Besties

Likes: Being brave; jumping up and down really fast

Dislikes: Waiting; mean kitty cats

Bella

Likes: Pretty things; shiny things

Dislikes: Brown things; broken things

Margo

Likes: Bugs; dancing

Dislikes: Balloons; courgette

Pickles

Likes: Sleeping; napping

Dislikes: Not sleeping; not napping

Abby Tabby